Love Letters to Strangers

By

A Brave Owl

ISBN: 9798835669998

Love Letters to Strangers

Love Letters to Strangers, III

Table of Contents

Dedication

Introduction

Chapter 1. Possible Again

Chapter 2. Flowers Shining in Falling Snow

Chapter 3. Hints of Change

Chapter 4. Flowers Slowly Return

Chapter 5. Thoughts of Love

Chapter 6. Bad Memories

Chapter 7. All These Wishes

Chapter 8. You and Me in the Shade

Chapter 9. Like All Dreams

Chapter 10. To Be Free

Chapter 11. The Things They Still Had Left

Chapter 12. The Best Place for Miracles

Afterword

Acknowledgments

About the Author

Love Letters to Strangers, V

Dedication

This book is dedicated
to you.

I don't know you
and I will never meet you, but

I love you.

Because,
you're a human,
like me,

and you
deserve to be loved.

Love Letters to Strangers, VII

Introduction

My Friend,

This book is about you. On Tiktok, Instagram, and Twitter, I made the whole wide world a deal.

"Tell me about yourself, and I'll write a poem about you."

In comments, in stories, in poems, and in pictures, you told me about yourself. And I wrote these poems about you.

Friendship. Love. Loss. Violence. Hope. Resilience. Faith. These are poems of the heart. Poems th were lived.

This book is my love letter to the whole world and to you.

If you want me to write the next poem about yo find me on Tiktok or Instagram @abraveowl

- A Brave Owl

P.S. If you can find the time, as an independent author I would much appreciate a short, honest review of this book on Amazon and/or Goodreads. Thank you <3

Love Letters to Strangers,

Chapter 1.

In January
everything was
possible again.

You send your heart
out into the world
like a bird.
"Fly to your home,"
you say. Even though
you are not sure
home exists.

You are confused.
This love in you
is so pure and so good. Why
is it so hard
for it to find its place?
Why is it turned away so often?

Can you change your heart?
Can you take it in your hands,
like mud, like clay,
and shape it into something
that will fit better
in this cruel world? But,
no.
Love is only love.
It cannot be counterfeit.

This is not your home.
You have not found it yet.
But I know
it is already waiting for you and you
are already good enough for it.

Through sunlight,
through wind and rain,
and heavy snow.
Through moon and star light.
Your heart flies on.

-        Your Heart is a Bird

She didn't want to be anyone
but herself.
She wanted to let her heart grow
its own way, like a vine,
sometimes crooked
and crawling,
but always reaching

-      For the Light.

She was not in control.
She knew it. Still,
she found it hard to let go.
The world was always changing,
through rarely how she hoped.

She kept her space clean.
She brushed her hair as if
to soothe herself.
She ordered her heart
with art, poetry, moonscape, sunset.

The world was made up of small things,
after all,
and at least these small things
she could care for
and keep safe.

"I'll start here" she thought,
holding her own heart
in her hand
like a glass.

She wanted to make the world
a better place, and
however small
she was a piece of this world

and she
would make herself
sturdy
and good.
She was in control
of herself.

    -    Where She Began

In her heart
she held the whole world.
But who
would hold her?

-      Looking for Someone to Hold

What did it mean
to have a heart.
To feel it beat in her chest.
What was all this existing for?
It was hard to have a heart, to keep it.
There must be a reason, a purpose.

Sometimes she felt lost,
the stars seemed distant, and small.

Her heart kept beating. sometimes

she was stubborn, and would not be moved
by anything in this world.

Her heart kept beating.

She did not know why
she had been given this life, but
it was hers now.
this heart was hers and
it kept beating.

    -    The Beat

In her dreams she lived
a hundred different love stories.
But in her life
she could never seem to find
the time for love.

She worked hard
to make her dreams come true.
Just not
her dreams of love.

That crystal place
beyond the stars.
The flaming core
at the center of the world.
Where did love come from?

Like reaching out
to grasp a piece
of an already faded dream,
she would sometimes wake up
crying.

She understood then
what was required of her.
A choosing of paths.
A fork in her heart.

In some ways
all of life is made up
of moments like these.
And choices like this.

Well.
Her first task
would be

-       To Trust Herself.

He was a soldier,
but he did not dream of war.

He liked poetry,
and the poets
of far away places.

Sometimes he dreamed
of other lives,
and sometimes he dreamed
of his own.

He carried a gun
and a book in his pocket,
and what made him
a good soldier,
he imagined, was that he
never gave up.

-      Dreams of Peace

She liked to wonder
and the feeling of lightness
that wonder gave her.
She didn't let the small things
weigh her down.

She could talk to anyone.
She could learn from anyone.
Every heart had a story
and she liked to draw them out
like snails out of shells.

Sometimes she wanted a reason
beyond the used up heartbeats
collecting in her body like fallen feathers.
Why? Why does the sun set that way?
Why does life go on and on?

What was it all for?
These relationships she made carefully
with her hands, like clay bowls.
But love felt like its own reason.
But her life felt like its own reason.

Perhaps God
does not deal in why.
Perhaps God
does not let the small things
weigh him down.

Maybe wonder is enough.

-    The Wondering Girl

Chapter 2.

The porch lights glowed
in February, like flowers
shining in the falling snow.

She couldn't sleep, but
she still had dreams.
Only the stars knew her wishes.
Only the moon knew her heart.

Sometimes she wondered
if she preferred the darkness,
the nighttime, because she
did not like to be seen.

Sometimes she dreamed about the sun,
hot light falling like water on her skin.
She liked children
and she made them laugh and feel safe.
She was a kind person
wasn't she?

The moon is never afraid
to be seen. The stars
are always shining.
She, too, had a light on in her heart.

To know our own hearts
we must share them.
The same way the starlight
is only known when it falls
softly upon on us
like snow.

- Nighttime Girl

Though she had lost
so much
there was still something
alive
inside her.

-      Human

She wrote poetry
like sending up
smoke signals
or prayers.

Like putting pieces
of her own heart
into tiny bottles
and giving them
to the sea.

Someday, she hoped,
someone would find them, read them.

She wanted to be seen
and to see.
She wanted to complete
the half finished puzzle
of her heart.

Surely someone's heart
fit here
beside hers.

She was in love.
and all she really wanted
was someone
to share that feeling with.

    -    Why She Writes

Life is a rough ride.
You're bound to lose
a few things on the way.
Learn to love the holes
and the whole. Learn to let the air
sing in the empty places.
Some things, once lost,
shall never return. But
new things
will always rise
if we let them.

-      The Holes And The Whole of Life

How to be good.
This was the puzzle of her life.
She understood
there were great forces
all around her.
From the Great Unknown
to the old rush hour traffic
to the virus.
To the golden hour
just before twilight.
To true love.
She was only a part of this world,
but she wanted to be responsible anway.
Well, she would have to trust her heart
to guide her.

-      How to be Good

You love the way
they glide through life.
Their easy smile,
and the way the sunlight
wraps around them like
an embrace.
Some people are loved
even by the stars.

You love them too. Yes.
You only wonder why
this world is so unfair.

Sometimes the shadows
other people cast
are so deep
you fear
you will drown in them.

And you wonder, too,
if all the stars love them,
then who is left
to love you?

Well.
No matter what comparisons
have been made
you cannot be them.
You can only be you.

But there is
enough light in this world
for you too.
Come out of the shadow
and see.

-    Your Shadow, Your Light

Sometimes you feel like an egg.
But even though
you are still becoming yourself
even an egg
must face the world
and live in it
and find a way
to love itself.

-       What's Inside That Shell, Friend?

Her heart fluttered
like a small bird.
The world was both huge
and fragile.

And if she let it go,
it would break.
Sometimes, she forgot
how to breathe.

Sunlight fell as heavy
as water.
her bird heart
sang.

She was so tired, but
she could not fall asleep

because, if she did
everything
would fall apart.

When she finally
had to rest,

her fingers uncurling
like dying leaves
in reverse,

the tightness in her heart
softening like cream,

when she finally
let go
everything
was okay.

   -   It's Okay to Rest

Love Letters to Strangers, 20

Chapter 3.

March was
still cold, but
in the lightning storms
and flurries of late snow
you start to see
hints of change.

Inside her was a dual nature.
She wanted adventure,
but needed a rest.
She was curious about the taste of sky
but lacked the confidence to take a bite.

Sometimes her body
betrayed or ignored her.
She tried to love herself,
as she loved the world,
and it's beckoning horizons.

Like twisted bed sheets,
sometimes breathing was a nightmare.
There was a warm space
between who she was
and who she wanted to be.

She wanted a bigger heart.
She did love herself,
and still longed for change.
Sometimes she wrote down
all the places she wanted to explore.

Today was the day
she put down her own name.
Like wild land, with its own wild sky
her heart was a place
of adventure and wonder.

Waiting to be explored.

-      Time for an Adventure

He only wanted to grow.
He was tired
of being small.
He worked the soil of his heart
like a field.
He still felt small.
He knew he would not change overnight.
He gave his heart
water and light
and one day he noticed, yes,
he was

- Growing.

She was learning
how strong she really was.
She world often asked her
to be strong.
Like holding up the sky.
She tried to believe in herself.

Outside, the sky was falling.
The old forests burned. The oceans rose.
She belonged to this world
and felt responsible for it,
which was why her heart
was always breaking.

Did it make her stronger,
she wondered,
to hurt so much?
It took strength to stand
to make a space for herself
in this world, in her own life.

Sometimes other people
tried to take her spirit.
When they had none of their own.
Still, she found it easy
to love this world.
Harder to love herself.

If any home can stand forever,
under any burning sky,
it is this home.
Her own body.
But she had a strong spirit.
So even if the sky did fall
she would be alright.

-      To Be Strong

He felt under the weather.
A heavy feeling, like being buried
under the clouds.

He was sick. Well.
Everybody got sick sometimes.
The whole world
got sick sometimes.

Well. This would not stop him,
just as other obstacles had not.
He had a will like thunder,
and a heart strong as the sun.

and this would not stop him.

-      Recovering

Her parents had cages
where their hearts used to be.
She dreamed of escape,
but her father told her
to forget her dreams.

Fear and anger and loneliness
swirled in her like a storm.
When people grew up
did their hearts always
turn into cages?

Forget your dreams.
Forget yourself.
Close your heart like a door
and make this whole
beautiful and terrible world
into your prison.

In her dreams she met herself again.
She touched her own heart.
"This is a prison
made out of pain."

She was only human.
She loved her parents.
She only wanted them to be happy
and free. But there were
some dreams, yes,
she had to let go of.

She would grow
into her own person.
She would grow strong
and forgive them,
and free herself.

    -    Forgiveness

Her moods came like weather.
She was a host of seasons.
Hot mornings in winter.
Cool storms in spring.
She loved food.
She loved the transformation
of many ingredients into one whole.
This was the stuff of life.
Transformation.
And she was

-       Alive

Chapter 4.

In April
the flowers
slowly returned.

When he danced
something was set free
inside him.
He rode the music
like a bird riding the wind.
It could take him anywhere.

He had always wanted
to see the world,
to hold it in his hands, gently.
Like something alive.
He wanted to go
anywhere. Everywhere.

But it was a time in the world
when things were shrinking,
and he was trapped
in this room, in this body,
in this, forever repeating, moment.

But when he danced
he wasn't in his body,
or his body wasn't in the room.
He was free.
He was dancing on the moon.

Or anywhere in the world.
When he danced
he was free.

- Dancer

He made websites for a living.
He hustled.
Cyber space
was not real space,
but people still lived there.
He was a home builder,
of sorts,
and like others
he had done bad but,
he only wanted to do good.

-       Cyber Hustler

Most stories are about change.
When she looked at herself
she saw her home,
and the long history of home
that had delivered her here.

India is a land of many poets,
and open hearts
of other kinds,
of which hers
was only the most recent.

She loved the curve of stone,
the arch of a doorway
like the smooth line of a lover's brow.
In her heart she was one thing.
In her life she was many.

History had taught her
that the world is always changing.
Even stone can be formed into a door.
She wanted to bend that change
like a river. She wanted the whole world.

Poets often have dreams
that are too big for their hearts.
And so their hearts
break open
and spill out
across the world
like ink.

-     A History of Home

A lonely heart, but
a beautiful one.
Open like a hand.
You feel
so much.
And everything
you have ever felt
you carry still.
It's heavy, isn't it?
But that's how it is
with hearts like yours.
You have a hard time
trusting people,
but you do trust people.
you're afraid of love,
but you love anyway.
You want let go of the past
but you hold on.
Open up that heart,
that beautiful
and lonely heart,
and let go.

-      You Deserve to be Light

She grew up strange,
crooked like a tree
reaching for the sky.
She held on
to her talismans
to feel safe.
She held on
to everything.

She collected her problems
in her mind
like butterflies in a net.
Sometimes she talked
to herself
just to fill the silence.

Do not misunderstand.
She was not a sad person.
She loved music.
She loved her friends
and her life, she
was only a little afraid
of change.

She was learning to let go,
to hold on.
She was learning
that her heart
could open and close like a hand.

She was learning
that life
would take much from her
but that it would
give much to her
as well.

    -    Open, Close

Everything they loved
felt very far away.
When people looked at them,
they saw somebody else.

Sometimes they imagined
what it might feel like
to disappear.
To fade into the light
like a ghost of themselves.

The truth was
maybe nobody really knew them.
But they were still here.
They were as real
as the moon,
or the earth,
or the ocean.

They just wanted
to grow up.
To grow strong,
in their heart.
But, like all real transformations,
it would take time.

Until then, they tried
to find enough love
in their own heart

    -    To Live.

He only wanted the world
to be beautiful.
Poetry was a cleansing space.
After writing a poem
his heart felt cleaned
and light again.
What is our purpose, and
how do we do good?
He was a teacher. He
directed hearts like flocks of birds.
While teaching, he had discovered
that you cannot save people.
You cannot shape people like clay.
Clay is not alive. Like poetry
his students lived. They suffered
and they loved.
They were living poems.
And beauty, in the end,
was anywhere he looked for it.

- 	Everybody's Got Some Place to Care For

She felt like her heart
was a wild horse that she rode.
She could not wait
for the world to be better.
It had to be better now.
Goodness was a war, for her,
like love.
Her heart had broken
as many times as it beat.
But she did not have time
for regret.
she rides on.

-    Fighter

"Who are you?"
She wasn't sure.
She made faces in the mirror
trying them on
like masks.

At night she dreamed
about her true self.
Rare as flowers on the moon
beautiful as stardust
falling like snow.

It sometimes felt as if
she was the only person
on this whole earth
who could see
herself.

She was real.
She had a body,
a heart. And this space
her body occupied
was hers alone.

This was her body.
This was her heart.
She was already
her true self. Even if
only she knew it.

-      True You

Chapter 5

Spring came to an end
in May. All hearts turned
to thoughts of love.

Her moods rose
like the ocean.
They fell like night.
She might open her mouth
and tear apart the sky.
She might reach out her hand
and hold all the world
like a child.
Her heart had a range
like an instrument.
Play it this way
and she'll laugh.
Play it this way
and she'll make you cry.
All people have their range
and must discover how
to play the music
in their own hearts.

-    It's a Mood

Their thoughts were loud
and sometimes chaotic,
and sometimes deceitful.
So, they decided, their voice
had to be louder
and truer.

\-   Be Loud

When asked about themselves
they thought about their name.
The Moon. The Gift of God.
This did not say much about them really,
and still it rang in their heart.

They were a literal person,
but also compelled by beauty.
They were introverted
and very cautious with their heart,
though they, too, longed to fall in love.

The moon, child, hangs above us all.
It belongs to no one,
and has no use for names.
Poetry too,
belongs to no one.

Be free with your heart.
Make a gift of your life.
For whom does this heart beat,
if not for you?
My moon child, my gift of god.

Shine like the moon.
Be dark like the moon.
Be near like the moon,
Be far like the moon.
Be loved
like the moon.

-    Hey There, Moon

He did not want to be judged,
but he wanted to be seen.
At night he looked for the moon.
During the day,
he made himself smile.
Most people he met
would never know who he was.
And fewer still
would touch his heart.
To be seen was to be misunderstood.
To be loved was to work through it.
To be protected, always,
was to be alone.
All people are judged, in life,
he knew, but
all people are also deserving

-      Of Love.

She had seen violence
in her time.
She knew its form and shape,
like an old boyfriend's smooth face.

Does violence erase love?
Yes
things do change.
That old boyfriend

had changed the shape
of her heart forever.
But, though battered,
her heart was still beating and

-      Capable of Love

Everybody was born under some star.
His were crossed like eyes.
Talent is nothing
without commitment.

Love is nothing
but a fistful of ashes
and an eternity of pressure.

Everybody blessed
and cursed
themselves.

He was of two minds.
Sometimes he felt
he got in his own way.

Sometimes he felt
like a supervillain,
and no one else in this world
could stop him.

Sometimes he felt
like a god.

But he was only a man.

- 　　Blessings, Blessings for All

First they were made
to wear dresses
that did not fit.
To wear eyeliner and blush
that made them look
like somebody else.

The soul has no face.
No clothes.
No gender.
No questions.
It only is.

Like chiseling away
the excess stone
to reveal the smooth
cool skin
of a Greek statue,
they found themselves
underneath themselves.

They were not the story
other people told about them.
They were the story
They wrote themselves,
the story they lived.

We cannot ever be
anyone but ourselves.
The chrysalis of our life
produces the butterfly
of our soul.

And after
all we need to do
is fly.

-      Who They Are

She was always moving
closer to who she would be tomorrow,
further away
from who she used to be.
and she was
always herself.

-      You Are

Chapter 6

It was already getting hot
in June. People shed layers
of clothes like old skin or
bad memories.

She was still waiting
for the fire
to pass through her heart.
Life had not gone
as she had hoped,
but she
was not ready to give up
on life or
on love.

-    A Lover

Some days were good
and some bad.
Both she filled with music.
Love was never such a bad thing,
but hers always seemed to vanish
like stars erased by the dawn.
Love was strange and so was beauty.
Ugliness
was a function of the seer,
not the seen. She knew this.
She was a poet and a musician.
Sometimes she sang in her dreams,
and sometimes she dreamed
while still awake.

-      The Musician

You're going far away
to find yourself.
You never quite feel prepared,
do you? but you
can't wait any longer.

The distance between
who you are
and who you want to be
feels greater than the distance
between the earth and the moon.
A chasm.

You worry too
that when you leave home behind,
it will change without you,
and vanish like smoke,
and you will have no place
to return to.

You are afraid and uncertain.
It's alright. Know
that you carry a piece of your home
buried in your heart like a seed
along with everything else
that you have ever loved.
You travel light.

You are a brave person.
You will learn who you are,
and so much more,
and when you do
you will look back and see that,
like the earth rising
though a sea of stars, you
were always ready.

  - To Leave Home

He saw himself as the victim.
Maybe it was true.
He had been victimized.
But when asked
to describe himself
he could not think
of a single good thing to say.

The wind in his dreams
told him secrets about himself.
He was strong, smart, and brave.
But when he woke up
these dreams always
faded quickly.

His family made him feel small.
The world swallowed him
like a cage.
He just wanted someone
to believe in him,
to see him
as he really was.

But how did he see himself again?
In his dreams he stood
in front of a mirror.
It was his bare soul
that looked back.
He could be
anything he wanted to be.

He was tired.
Life would grind him to dust
if he let it.
He could not change
how other people saw him.
But he could change
how he saw himself.

Just as night
gives to day,
his heart
was changing.

\-   The Victim

Why was art
the closest thing she had
to prayer?

Draw me a picture
of my heart,
then set it on fire.
Let the smoke take it
all the way to heaven.
Sing me a song,
and I'll close my eyes and listen.

Was art the same thing as love?
Was real art like real love,
rare and beautiful?
Then why did it feel
as if art was the only thing
tethering her soul to this world?

What would it take
to really become herself, an artist?

She sometimes felt like a ghost
wrapped in fleshy baggage.
But this body,
she knew, she knew,
was a kind of art too,
just like her life was.

Art does not have to be good.
It only needs a heart to believe in it.
It only needs a heart

to call its home.
even if that heart
was only her own.

-      Artsy Lady

She wanted to be read, to be loved,
like a good book.
She wanted the mystery of herself
to linger in someone's mind
like the scent of peach perfume
left behind
in the shared backseat of a Lyft.
She wanted to be looked at like the moon,
wondered at like the stars. Known
like the sun. But she
did not like revealing herself,
and sometimes wondered if
she needed to be brave,
and worry less
about who would read her life story
and more about who
would write it.

-    The Writer

There was something romantic
about being lost.
The ocean, at night,
was as dark as a starless sky.
There were wild places left
everywhere.
They were only hiding.
In strange pools left behind at low tide
like the ocean's stray children.
In the shadows of the streets.
In the blades of grass
tangling between her toes
like fingers.
It was a complicated world,
but a beautiful one
to be lost in.

-    It's Still a Beautiful Place, Earth

It was a season of despair.
In the world, and
in her heart. She
kept her hopes buried
deep in the soil of her chest,
strange seeds.

Sometimes she imagined
she could close her eyes
and stop the world like
breaking a clock, but
the world is always moving.
Just like her heart.

She was alive, and life
never stops.
She was scared, but
she was also brave.

She kept her hopes buried
way down in her heart,
but she kept them

-      alive.

Chapter 7

July. Fireworks and
late nights. Warm red wine and
so many stars above.
All these wishes.
Some must come true.

Like comets
flying through outer space.
Like stars
falling out of the sky.
They just kept
missing each other.

Not all love
is meant to be.
Not all comfort
comes when we need it.
Find your center.
that hollow place
in your heart.

You are stronger
than this heartbreak.
There is room in your heart
for more than this.

In time,
this hollow space,
this holy place,
will fill with love again.

-       Your Heartbreak

She was not afraid to break.
She did not need beauty,
though she could sing, if called to.
Sometimes she held the pieces of herself,
and sometimes she let them go.

She rebuilds herself the same.
She rebuilds herself different.
At her center, that dusty place,
is her same old heart.
Sometimes

hearts ache.

It's just what hearts do.
And sometimes they sing.
Ask her, and she will tell you.
Love has a depth like no other place.
Some goodbyes hurt more than others.

Life will hurt you.
Your heart will break.
It's alright.
Heartbreak comes
with having a heart.

It's alright.
Ask her, and she will tell you.
Broken hearts
beat just the same.
And are no less deserving, or

-    Capable of Love.

She knows that,
during the fall,
there's no friction.
She's fallen before.

To fall in love
is to give up herself completely.
She wonders what it is to be whole
when she's always changing.

But with him it feels different.
But with him it feels real.
It feels like there's nothing missing
inside her anymore.

Maybe this time
she would land.

-        The Longest Fall, the Softest Landing

The heart makes its roots
deep in the body.
Love can be twisted,
and it can lead you places
you never expected to go.

He loved somebody,
and that was a beautiful thing.
As for her, well.
Love can be twisted.
Still, he didn't want to give up.

Even love has its sunset, and it's night.
His heart wouldn't let him give up,
even though he deserved more
than a half moon
and a nighttime lover.
But that
was all that he had.

    -    Nighttime Lover

Surely
there was someplace for her.
Someplace
beyond all the this
old pain.

-     Heal

You are lost in the starfall.
In the tall gray waves
that crash against the shore
of our age, endlessly,
scattering us like sand.
You are torn apart
like clouds in the sunlight.
You are not alone.

Everything falls.
Look around and see.
There is no person
on this whole earth
who has not felt pain.
Whose heart has not broken. It's
alright. We carry on
as best we can.
Close your eyes.

Find the slowness
of your heartbeat.
Humans are built to hurt. Yes.

But we are also built to love.

Find that love inside yourself.
It will be shaped like a seed.
Small. Hard.
And full of possibility.
It is not too late.
It is never too late.
To start loving yourself.
You may be lost,
but you are not gone.

  - You Are Still Here

He knew that people
carried their heartbreaks close,
like stones
weighing them down.

But he wanted
to let his go.
He wanted
to be light.

-      To Be Light

You cannot change
other people's hearts.
You cannot make
anyone love you.

The fires rage
all through the summer.
The cities flood
all across the globe.

The world shrinks into itself
like a lonely human soul,
and in your heart, it feels
like the end of the world.

In the morning
the birds still sing.
All over the world
people are still falling in love.

The only thing
that is truly yours
in this world
is your heart.

It is never broken
beyond repair.
It is never so lost
that it cannot be found.
It is your heart.

You cannot make
anyone love you.
You cannot change
other hearts.
But you can change yours.

    -    You're Changing Already

The world was often frightening.
She had a heart like glass,
fine and clear.
She wanted to understand someone
and be understood in return.
She had so much love to give,
but are were so few places
for love in this world.
To love then,
she understood,
she would need to be brave.

-      Be Brave

He was confident.
He had time to spend, and a young heart.
He fell in love easily,
and just as easily, he moved on.

He let life wash over him
like wind.
He loved the dirt as much as the sky.
Every minute was a new opportunity
to fall in love.

To fall out of love
he simply held his breath,
and closed his eyes,
and when he opened them,
there was always something new.

He was a simple man
with an unsteady heart.
Some people have to love
every last thing they see.
His heart hurt.

Sometimes it was just easier
to love somebody else,
to love the sky.
There was peace in nature,
even when there was none in his heart.

Someday, his heart would settle
as the moon settles
soft on the horizon.
And he would fall in love
for good.
And be brave enough
to keep it.

-      Time Spent on Love

Chapter 8

The full heat of the sun.
Sudden like a crime.
You and me in the shade, listening
to the August blues.

After sunset
you like to dance
in empty parking lots,
as if you can make friends
with the nighttime.
You wish it was easier
to make friends.

Sometimes you wear stories
putting on other lives
like coats. Sometimes it feels like
you are always dreaming.
This happens most
when you are alone.

You are a true friend.
If only there were more people
who knew it. Well.
The sun sets, and you
keep dancing.

-      A Friend

She had a date.
It was not particularly good
or particularly bad.
She wondered when love would come for her.

He had seemed concerned
about offending her.
He avoided heartfelt subjects,
like she did.

His heart had seemed
already full of someone else.
Someone he had once known,
or else, had only imagined.

She did not think of him again after.

-     Bad Date

It's hard to let go.
But your forgiveness
wasn't for them.
It was for you.
you
can let go of that weight.

  - Time to Move On

You feel alone,
even at parties.
You feel your heart
floating in this emptiness,
the same way the planets float
in the emptiness of space.
It is a cold
and vast feeling.

The stars seem very distant,
like wishes.
The wind never seems
to call your name.
You know you are not alone.
You know it, you just
can't feel it.

To have a friend,
you must first be a friend.
Do you love yourself?
Do you listen to yourself?
Are you there for yourself?

Come back to your heart.
that fist of muscle and flesh
always working
to keep you alive.

You are not alone.

Place your hand
over your heart
and feel it.

  - You Are Not Alone

He worried a lot
about monsters. He knew
anyone could be a monster.
He had seen good people
disintegrate
into shadows of themselves.
The heart was a strange egg,
which could hatch
into anything.
He wanted to be brave, but
it was a scary world.
Full of monsters.
But he would at least
keep his own heart
soft
and human.

-     Young Boy

She had a shell
like layers of bone.
It was not a soft world,
and she had to live in it.
She wanted to speak. She wanted
to pour her heart into a glass
like wine for someone to drink.
From inside herself she watched
the world fall
like a star.

"Someone come here,"
she wished from inside.
"Someone come here,
and find me."
The only light
came through the cracks.
The only sound came
from her own heart.
"Here I am,"
her heart said,
softly.

-      Here I Am

Your heart is heavy.
Heavy as a stone
sinking into the sea.
It's alright.

Like a bird
flying free.
Like a star
falling out of the sky.

Let it out.

Because even though
it can be heavy,
your heart
is not a burden.

It is the place
where all love lives,
and all pain,
and it is a gift.

Some things
we cannot change,
but those things
we can share.

When love is shared
it grows greater.
When pain is shared
it grows smaller.

And when a heart is shared
it grows

   -   Lighter.

It was true.
Most every heart
had been broken.
It is the oldest story.
But each time
this story is lived
someone was brave
and chose hope
over fear.
She was such a girl.

-      A Brave Girl

Chapter 9

Like all dreams
summer came to an end.
September brought
a new chill to the air.

He was edgy.
he did not like
being at the edge of things, really.
But that was here he was.
The edge was not a safe place to be.

Before him, in the abyss,
all stories unraveled
like yarn. Like tragedy.
He had discovered that, in language,
there is no core.
It was as if the stars themselves
had gone out like candles.

Like others, he was searching.
Sometimes, it felt like being lost.
Sometimes the night sky
was still full of stars and meaning,
and a poem might make him weep.

There was no particular place to be.
He was here. Only lost if he imagined
he was supposed to be somewhere else.
What was so wrong, anyway,
with being human?

Not a thing. Not a thing.
We don't really find our way,
so much,
as we make our way.
Wherever we are.

    -    Lost, Not Forever

She had lived through disappointment,
but it only made her
more sure of her heart.
diner coffee, and bad eggs,
and old love songs
made her feel better.
She loved the cool
of things gone by. How smooth
memories were, even
if they had never really happened.
She had a heart like an old movie.
It felt
timeless.
She was sure
she would love again. It was as if
it had already happened.

-    Retro Romantic

He wondered if she
still thought of him,
like he thought of her.
It struck him
that he was not an important person.

His heart was full of missing things,
like bread crumbs he'd left behind,
to find his way home,
only to watch them be eaten
by wild birds.

Was it human
to hurt this much?

Of course it was.

The next day he felt better.
washed by sleep.
but then the way a woman floated
out of a restaurant
would make him think of her again.

Was this to be the rest of his life?
The next day he woke up
with a headache.
The next day
he didn't think of her at all.

Time had a way of passing.
One day he realized,
he could no longer hear her laugh.
in his mind,
and he laughed out loud.

He did not want to forget.
He wanted to be important
to somebody. But he had
his own life to live, too.
Even if he tried to stop his heart

Time would keep on moving.
It was human to forget.
And it was human to heal.
It was human to fall in love again.
Someday. Someday.

-       You're Important to Me.

Life takes away
pieces of our hearts,
like stones lost
down a wishing well.
She knew
what it was to lose.

Everyday she woke up
from wild dreams
she mostly could not remember.
Was she falling, or flying?
Singing, or crying?
She checked her heartbeat.
Yes. she was still here.

Time passed.
Her battered heart
kept on beating.
She found that even
with missing pieces,
hearts keep growing.

No heart is worth more
than another.
And all hearts
grow different,
and break different,
and heal different.

There was nothing wrong
with her.
Her heart was more
than good enough.
Her heart was good.

-    Good Hearted Girl

He was always falling in love.
Sometimes he thought about the stars
and the way they fell
through the dark forever.
Like a leaf, it is the nature of a star
to fall.

He did his best
to take care of himself.
He did not like being a burden.
His heart was a weight,
and he would carry his own weight.

The stars were always silent and beautiful
and faraway.
But stars do not have hearts.
It was hard to ask for help,
hard to show his heart, but

to be loved
you must first be seen.
And you cannot be seen
until you show yourself.

He was not a star.
He was a human being.
His nature was to love, and to be loved,
and to show his heart
and let someone help him
carry that weight.

    -    The Weight of a Heart

She did not love herself.
Others had used her like a doll.
Stepped on her heart
and let it fall. So
she had to make it harder.
Like a stone.

It was not fate
that kept love from her.
It is the destiny
of every human soul
to love.

But, when so many faces
stared through her
as if she was made of glass
when so many hands
moved past her
without touch
when so many people
left her behind
taking all
her love with them
it was hard to find any left
for herself.

No one can save you
if you cannot save yourself first.
No one can love you
if you cannot love yourself first.

There was still a well inside her,
endlessly deep and giving.
Cool and clean water
and stillness
like a soul.

-      "Love Yourself First"

In the storm
she met herself again,
like an old friend
She'd almost forgotten
who she was.

-      A Woman Like a Storm

Love Letters to Strangers, 93

Chapter 10

In October
even ghosts
are allowed
to be free.

Sometimes she still
found him
in unexpected corners
of her heart.

It was a surprise
to find that
she still missed him.

Like flowers
and wild grasses
growing back after a fire

it would take
a little longer
for the missing pieces of her
to return.

-      Breakups

Fall leaves lifting off the ground
and back onto their branches,
like mistakes undone.
The story of her life
was moving backwards.
She had fallen out of love.

She liked the hard gray of the ocean
and days heavy with fog.
The soft gray of a full moon
made her think of old movies
and dancing under the light of silver screens.
She was a lonely kind of romantic.

There was something cracked
in her heart.
Sometimes it hurt to smile.
She wanted to be in love, yes,
but first she would have to find some way
to love herself.

She would go back to the beginning.
Let the whole world turn back
like a broken clock,
like the sun setting in the east and rising in the west,
when she had been young
she had been so full of love.

That self was still alive
somewhere inside her.

-        Inner Child

Even love changes.
She wanted to transform
her feelings into art
so that the art might feel
all this pain
instead of her.

She didn't know what to do
and to accept that sometimes
nothing can be done
felt impossible.

Her tears were real.
She was stuck in love like
a fossil buried in cool earth
for millions of years. It is true.
Love never ends.

But it does change.

- Where do All These Tears Go?

Love asked
much of him.
But he
always answered.

-    Lover Boy

She was strong.
Sometimes her heart
felt newborn.
Soft, loud. Easily bruised
at a touch.
But the ability to feel
so much
was not a weakness.
Love filled her like a storm. Joy
washed away her fear. Pain
was deeper
than all the empty space
between the stars,
and between people.
Friendship felt like
the whole world
and all of time
held in her heart like small,
warm fire.
Was this weakness?
Or was it just
realness.

-      A Real One

This was
her one life.
It had to be
enough.

-     It's All We Have

Although she
was sometimes alone,
loneliness
did not define her.

She only felt
as others did.

With the whole
of her heart.

-      Lonely? Only Sometimes

Some stories end.
But hearts, like yours,
are resilient.

Some people will leave you behind.
For others,
you will be the one who leaves.

Not all things stay,
it's true.

But know that
in your heart
lives all that you
have ever loved.

Wherever life takes you,
hold on to your heart.

Like a compass,
it will always lead you home.

-      Heartfelt Advice

Chapter 11

In November they were grateful
for the fallen leaves
and close gray skies,
and for all of the things
they still had left.

What she really struggled to do
was love herself.

The clouds in the sky
never wonder
if they are beautiful.

The mountains have no mirrors.
The wind has no body.

The birds sing
because it is
their nature to sing.

These things are beautiful
because they exist, and

because they are always themselves.

She too
was herself,
and beautiful,
and loved.

-    The Clouds Never Wonder

It was hard
to make them listen.
It was harder
to stop speaking.

There was something inside her
growing like a universe.
There was a melody
on her mind like a life vest.

Silence was her enemy.
She had a loud heart.
She wondered, at times,
if other people felt this way.

-    Pretty Voice

She was raised to be
a perfect no one.
A face as calm and
expressionless
as a blank summer sky.
But she felt more
like a storm. Like a someone.

There were so many rooms
in her heart
that even she
did not know them all.

She was finding that life and living,
was messy and beautiful.
The only perfect things
were dead things.
She only wanted
to live her life.

She was a prism.
She broke the pale,
soft light of living
into every color.
She was not blank.

She could not be
no one.
She could only be
herself.

-    Somebody Real

Her world was
a balance of opposites.
She liked day better
when it was night.
She felt lonely
in a crowd.

She was looking
for connection.
She wanted
to change the world.
Don't we all?

She kept all her troubles
sealed tight in glass jars,
where she could
study them closely
without ever
opening the jar.

She smiled through the pain.
She drifted
in her own mind
like outer space,
swimming in the stars.

Set yourself free.
Unseal your heart
from its jar.
Sometimes she felt
like she was alone.
But she was not alone.

-      Connections

She had known violence,
and violence
had known her.
It was not her fault.

Years fell
like snowflakes,
softly.
She had been healing
for a long time.

The world was
not a fair place.
The world was
not a kind place.

This is why
she was kind in her heart.
This is why
she was fair in her soul.

She watched her child grow.
She worked her own heart,
like clay. She said,
"You can be
anything you want to be."

This was not the heart
she expected, but
it was
the heart that she had.

And there was no violence
is this world
that could destroy it.

- D.V.

The weather in your heart
was never steady.
A storm has just passed, or else
there is one on the horizon.
You smell burning ozone
and the freshly torn earth.

You find that
no matter how clearly
you map out your own heart,
your own soul, in words,
in stories and in poems,
you cannot seem to find
the answer.
Where do you belong?

Sometimes there is
so much inside in you,
and other times
the emptiness stretches out,
scattered starcape and held breath.

Wherever you are
you must first find a way
to belong in your own skin.

If you need to let it out,
then let it out.
If you need to hold on,
then hold on.

There is no such thing
as a final answer.
But isn't this life,
and all its strange moods,
still quite beautiful?

    -    An Answer

There was a picture of her
in her own mind. Smiling
like she knew a secret. Smooth
as sunset and rose wine. Unafraid,
like the sky.

This was the person
she was supposed to be.

She watched the days of her life
burn away like candles.
Forgotten like old wishes.
She kept falling
further and further
behind the picture of herself.

What she feared had no name.
only a cold presence
like a shadow.
Always with her.

There is never any way to know
how much time we have left.
All she had for sure
was this moment.

Each day she lived.
It was not like in her dreams,
but it was real.

eventually she forgot
who she was supposed to be,
and became instead
herself.

-     A Picture of Her

The universe spins
like a top.
Days unfold slowly
like flowers.

In the middle of the night
the world is very silent, but
your heart is never silent.

How do you find your way home
when you have never been there?

You don't feel like yourself,
but then, you are not sure
who you are anyway.

Many paths
like worlds breaking apart
lead away from today.
Some end here.

Maybe it will never feel
as if you have found yourself.
But you are here.

Your heartbeat is a song
like no other in the world.
listen.

To be alive
is to be brave.
And I am so glad

-      You Are Still Here.

Chapter 12

December.
The end is always
the best place
for miracles.

She was struck by wonder as a child
like lightning.
It has never left her body.
She had a good imagination,
and knew a thousand ways
her life could have been better.
Like the tangled roots of a tree,
all the paths that could have been.
Sometimes, she felt like a cloud
blown by the wind. Sometimes
she felt like the rain,
falling everywhere.
Though in her heart
her thousand shadows danced,
in the world she had only
one life.

Perhaps there were better roads,
but we all must walk the paths under our feet.
The forks ahead have yet to be chosen,
but the ones behind are gone.

-	A Long Journey

Peace. Fulfillment. A place to belong.
Most of the things we search for
are not objects that can be bought,
nor are they feelings,
which can only come from our own hearts.

Peace is a relationship
with the world.

Belonging is a daily chore.

Fulfillment is a balancing act
with your heart on one side
and the world on the other.

To find these things
is to make them,
and always, always, always
be making them.

-      Making a Life

Isn't it exciting
to wake up everyday?
This is the moment
when all things are possible.

Maybe you will fall in love today, or
maybe you will fall out of love.

Maybe you will hear
the right poem
at the right time,
and, for a moment,
your heart will feel reborn.

Maybe today you will find
forgiveness in yourself.

Maybe today you think of someone
you have not thought of in years
and smile.

Maybe today
will be your better day.

-    Or Maybe Tomorrow

She liked to sleep.
it was while she slept
that the world was perfect.
Dreams never have edges
or any pain.

The world contained ugliness.
This was fact.
Sometimes she stared out the window
and saw her dreams roll by
instead of what was really there.

She was a survivor.
She survived her life.
She could find beauty
in the most torn apart places.
Everyone dreamed of a better world.

Dreams are a part of the world
just as much as stones.
Dreamers are not cowards,
they are survivors.
And they make the world

a kinder place.

   -   Somebody Else's Dream Girl

Sometimes she dreamed
that she was a flower.
breaking earth
and reaching for the sky
all her life.

She was at peace
with the heart of the world.
She understood
the cycle of all things.
Flowers grow, bloom,
and fade away.

The song of sunlight.
The melody of the moon.
Everyday was a gift,
and she
would not waste it.

-    Flower Girl

Their heart felt
squeezed.
They watched love
pass them by
like missing
the last train home.

They sometimes felt
out of step with the world.
A lagging audio track,
their lips never quite catching up
to the words
they really wanted to say.

"I love you."

Moments slipped through their fingers,
like water.
Their heart felt tight. They
just kept missing.

Sometimes love is hard.
And some love
is not meant to be.
But their heart
was made to love.

There was a sudden softening
in their chest. They understood.
Life is long.

There would be lots of people
in their life
who would love them,
just for them.
There will be.

    -    I Promise

They felt better
in their own skin
than in
anyone else's.

    -    Transitioning Into Yourself

What was it about life
that made her want
to escape it?
She dreamed of herself, only,
happier.

She dreamed of parties
at the bottom of the ocean.
She dreamed of revolution
in the heart of the world.
She dreamed of love.

There was no place
for her or her dreams
in this dying world.
She could not be happy
in this empty hearted place.

Life is not a dream, but
the world is changing.
She could not escape,
but she could change.
Maybe

If she scattered her dreams
like a fistfuls of seeds
all across this world
something new
could grow.

-       Dreamseeds

He was a positive person
by nature. By circumstance
He was a realist.
Life always seemed able
to get harder. Still he
was a believer to the end.

Beautiful things made him calm.
The water reaching for the sky
at the edge of the world. Waves
as gentle as his breathing.
He had learned how to take peace
from a good meal.

Life was way out of control.
He sometimes felt
the world collapsing in on itself,
like an ancient house
finally surrendering to the earth.

All he could do was live a good life.
As good a life as life allowed.
He was a friend to his friends,
a lover to his lovers,
and a human being to the world,
which he loved
despite the pain it brought him.

Sometimes he felt he deserved more.
Yes. Indeed he did.
But he would not allow himself
to be haunted by what should have been.
He had fought ghosts before,
and had banished them all.

If he was free nowhere else,
he was free in his heart.
If there was love nowhere else,
then there was love in his heart.
All he needed to do
was be true to his own soul.

He was a believer in the end.
He believed in himself.

-       Believer

Afterword

My Friend,

My hope is that this book brought a little more love and a little peace into the world and into your life.

Every human heart that is still beating is a poem in motion in the world, and I only tried to capture that here.

This book contains over 100 poems about strangers I met in digital spaces. But I could just as easily have written these poems about you. If you saw yourself in any of these poems, it is because we all share human hearts. The heartbeat is one of our oldest and most powerful poetic forms.

Whether someone has written it down or not, your life is a poem.

Thank you for sharing it with me.

Writing this book has taught me, all over again, that poetry is all around us. All it needs is someone to believe in it.

Thank you for believing in this book. Your next task is to believe in yourself.

Love hard, live brave, and be kind to yourself.

- A Brave Owl 2022

P.S. If you want me to write the next poem about you, find me on Tiktok or Instagram @abraveowl

P.P.S. If you can find the time, as an independent author I
would much appreciate a short, honest review of this book
on Amazon and/or Goodreads. Thank you <3

Love Letters to Strangers,

Acknowledgments

My deepest thanks to all those people who were brave and told me about themselves. You all have beautiful souls. Thank you for sharing a piece of them with me. I hope you liked your poems!

Thanks also to my followers and the many readers and viewers who interacted with or even silently read these poems in their first draft forms as I posted them on social media. The writing of this book was a journey we took together. I would have been lonely without you.

Thanks to my friends, especially Joy and Jair, who I also wrote about in this book. You too were brave and opened your hearts to me for the sake of poetry. I could not be more grateful.

Finally, and always, thank you to my wife, my starlight, Elsa. For everything.

About the Author

A Brave Owl has published three other books, most recently the poetry collection *Lullabies in Starlight.* He has both a Bachelor's and a Master's degrees in Creative Writing and English. He teaches High School English for living in Sacramento, California, where he lives with the love of his life. You can find him online on Tiktok or Instagram @abraveowl